T0413787

SPACE SCIENCE

Satellites and Space Probes

By Sophie Washburne

Cavendish
Square

Library of Congress Cataloging-in-Publication Data

Names: Washburne, Sophie, author.
Title: Satellites and space probes / Sophie Washburne.
Description: Buffalo, NY : Cavendish Square Publishing, [2024] | Series:
The inside guide. Space science | Includes bibliographical references
and index.
Identifiers: LCCN 2023031066 | ISBN 9781502670229 (library binding) | ISBN
9781502670212 (paperback) | ISBN 9781502670236 (ebook)
Subjects: LCSH: Artificial satellites–Juvenile literature. | Space
probes–Juvenile literature.
Classification: LCC TL796.3 .W37 2024 | DDC 629.46–dc23/eng/20230713
LC record available at https://lccn.loc.gov/2023031066

Editor: Jennifer Lombardo
Copyeditor: Jill Keppeler
Designer: Deanna Lepovich

Find us on

CONTENTS

This map shows the countries that were part of the Soviet Union.

1 RUSSIA
2 ESTONIA
3 LATVIA
4 LITHUANIA
5 BELARUS
6 UKRAINE
7 MOLDOVA
8 GEORGIA
9 ARMENIA
10 AZERBAIJAN
11 KAZAKHSTAN
12 UZBEKISTAN
13 TURKMENISTAN
14 KYRGYZSTAN
15 TAJIKISTAN

Chapter One

THE FIRST SATELLITES

During World War II (1939–1945), the United States and the Soviet Union were **allies**. However, there were many things they did not agree on. By the end of the war, both countries had grown powerful. Neither country trusted the other; each was worried the other would attack. To stop this from happening, each country tried to show that its military and **technology** were the strongest. This competition became known as the Cold War, and space played a big part in it.

The Space Race

The Space Race was part of the Cold War. Both the Americans and the Soviets wanted to be the first to put a person on the moon. Because they were competing, they each quickly achieved a lot.

Fast Fact

In 1922, the country of Russia joined with several other countries to become the Union of Soviet Socialist Republics (USSR), often called the Soviet Union.

The U.S. military had a big lead on the Soviets. This was mainly because they brought scientists from Nazi Germany to the United States to work on the space

This picture from July 24, 1950, shows the first rocket launched from Cape Canaveral, Florida.

program. The Nazis had already been working on rockets, and these scientists brought their knowledge with them. However, the Soviets managed to make some **breakthroughs** before the Americans.

Sputnik 1

The Soviets were the first people to put a satellite into space. A satellite is an object that orbits another object. It can be natural or man-made.

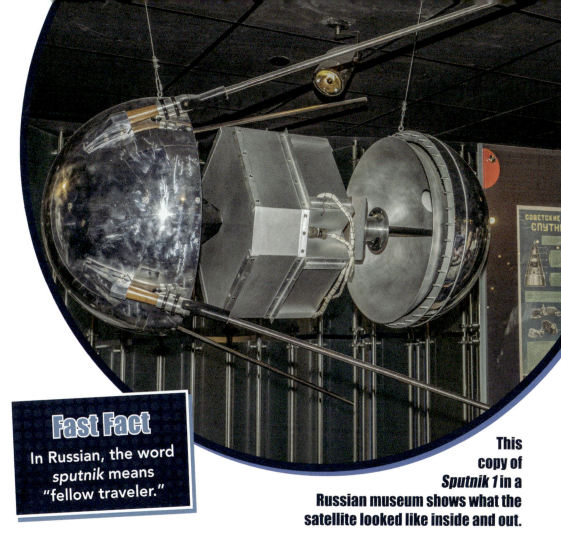

This copy of *Sputnik 1* in a Russian museum shows what the satellite looked like inside and out.

An example of a natural satellite is Earth's moon. The Soviets made a satellite they called *Sputnik 1*. It weighed 184 pounds (85 kilograms). It was made of metal and was about the size of a basketball.

On October 4, 1957, the Soviets launched *Sputnik* into orbit. It traveled around Earth at 18,000 miles (29,000 kilometers) per hour for three months. *Sputnik 1* had a radio **transmitter** on it that broadcast, or sent out, a beeping noise. It passed over the United States every 96 minutes, and people who had a certain kind of radio could pick up its beeps.

In January 1958, *Sputnik 1*'s orbit decayed, and it fell back to Earth, where it burned up in the **atmosphere**. All orbits decay over time. This means that satellites get closer to the object they're orbiting. The man-made satellites in our sky stay up for so long because people on the ground can control them remotely. The Soviet scientists didn't have a remote control for *Sputnik 1*, so they couldn't control when or where it crashed back to Earth.

There are many reasons why orbital decay happens. One of the biggest reasons is because of Earth's atmosphere. Atmospheric **particles** extend into space. When they hit a satellite, the satellite slows down just a little bit. Over time, it slows to a point where it can't stay up anymore.

Sputnik 2

In November 1957, the USSR launched *Sputnik 2*. This satellite held a dog named Laika— the first animal to orbit Earth. *Sputnik 2* included a camera that sent pictures back to Earth so the Soviets could watch Laika. With no way to get the satellite back down, the Soviets

Fast Fact

Sputnik 1 was too small to be seen from the ground. However, part of the rocket that got it into space followed *Sputnik*'s orbit and could be seen with **binoculars** when it was dark out.

This picture shows Laika, Earth's first orbital space traveler, before her launch.

knew she would die, so they only gave her enough food, water, and air for 10 days. However, the satellite was damaged after it reached orbit. The damage caused Laika to overheat and die sooner than planned. *Sputnik 2*'s orbit decayed after 162 days.

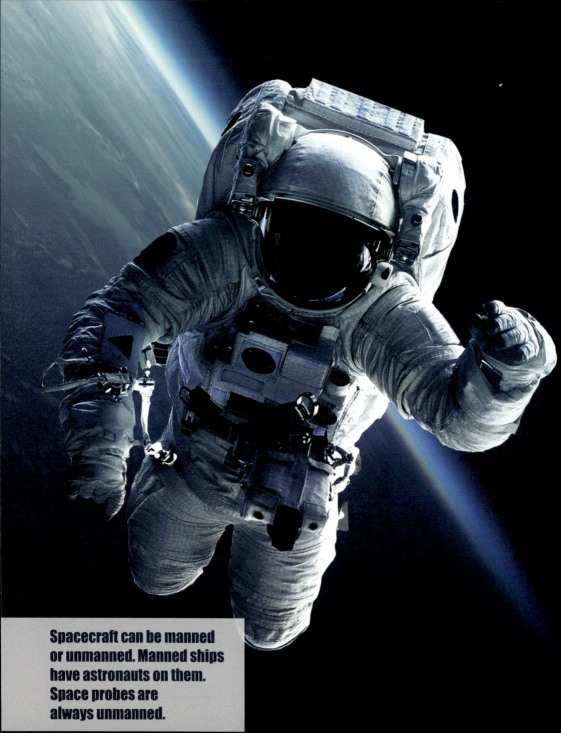

Spacecraft can be manned
or unmanned. Manned ships
have astronauts on them.
Space probes are
always unmanned.

SPACE EXPLORATION

*S*putnik 1 was not only the first satellite in history; it was the first space probe as well. A space probe is an object that is sent into space to gather information. It sends the information back to scientists on the ground on Earth. Space probes are a major way we've found out what we know about space today.

The Mariner Probes

As time went on, scientists continued to improve the technology they were working with. Between 1962 and 1973, the U.S. National Aeronautics and Space Administration (NASA) made 10 probes as part of a program called Mariner. They were meant to fly past Venus, Mars, and Mercury. The first and eighth probes were destroyed by accidents at launch time. A mistake caused the third probe to go off course, so it never reached Mars. However, the rest of the probes successfully completed their missions.

Fast Fact

Sputnik 1 had four long antennas. These recorded information about the **density** and temperature of the upper atmosphere—things it was impossible to measure from the ground.

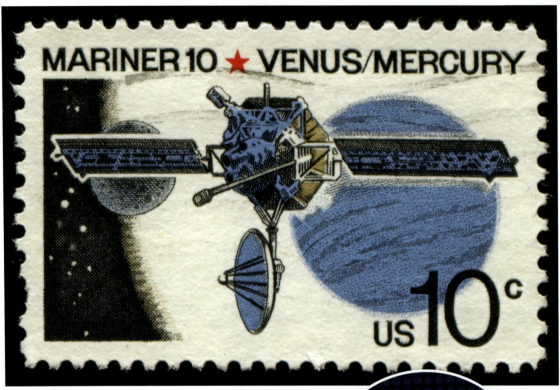

MARINER 10 ★ VENUS/MERCURY

US 10c

This stamp from 1975 shows
Mariner 10 on its way to Venus.

Thanks to the Mariner probes, scientists learned a lot about our three closest planets. They sent back photos, measurements of **cosmic** dust and solar wind, and information about the planets' atmospheres. For example, from *Mariner 2*'s trip in 1962, scientists learned that Venus's upper atmosphere is between -30 degrees and -70 degrees Fahrenheit

Fast Fact

Venus's thick atmosphere traps heat, making it the hottest planet in the solar system. On the surface, it's about 900°F (482°C).

(-34 degrees and -57 degrees Celsius) but the atmosphere then heats up quickly. Between the 1960s and 1980s, the Soviets launched a series of probes as part of the Venera program. Several of them landed on Venus's surface, where they were quickly destroyed by the heat and pressure of the atmosphere.

The Voyager Probes

In 1977, NASA launched two probes, *Voyager 1* and *Voyager 2*, at almost the

This picture shows the trajectories, or paths, of both Voyager probes.

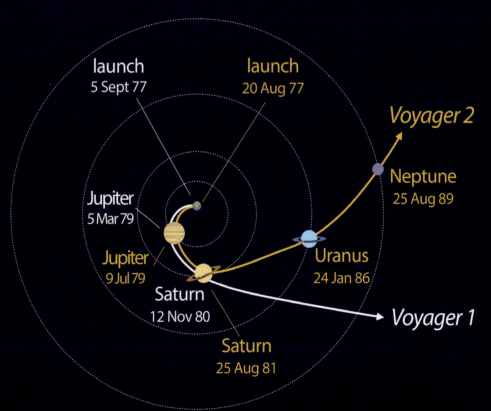

launch
5 Sept 77

launch
20 Aug 77

Voyager 2

Neptune
25 Aug 89

Jupiter
5 Mar 79

Jupiter
9 Jul 79

Uranus
24 Jan 86

Saturn
12 Nov 80

Voyager 1

Saturn
25 Aug 81

WHAT IS INTERSTELLAR SPACE?

The sun is constantly giving off particles and a magnetic field that travel into space at about 670,000 miles (1,078,260 km) per hour. This is called solar wind. Because the sun is so big, this solar wind affects space for a very long distance. The area that is affected is called the heliosphere. The place where the heliosphere stops is called the heliopause.

The heliopause is where interstellar space starts. It's hotter inside the heliosphere than outside of it because of the solar wind. When the Voyagers' instruments, or tools, started showing a drop in the temperature around them, scientists knew they had left the heliosphere. However, it will take about 30,000 more years for them to leave the solar system completely.

same time. The goal of the Voyager program was to explore interstellar space. The probes sent back the clearest pictures anyone had ever seen of some of the moons and planets in the outer solar system.

In 2012, *Voyager 1* entered interstellar space. Six years later, *Voyager 2* followed it. As of 2023, they're the only working spacecraft in interstellar space. They still collect information and send it back to Earth.

Each Voyager probe has something special on it: a golden record. The probes will stop working someday, but they'll stay in

The pictures on the golden record hold more information for any aliens. For example, the pictures on the top left show how the record is supposed to be played.

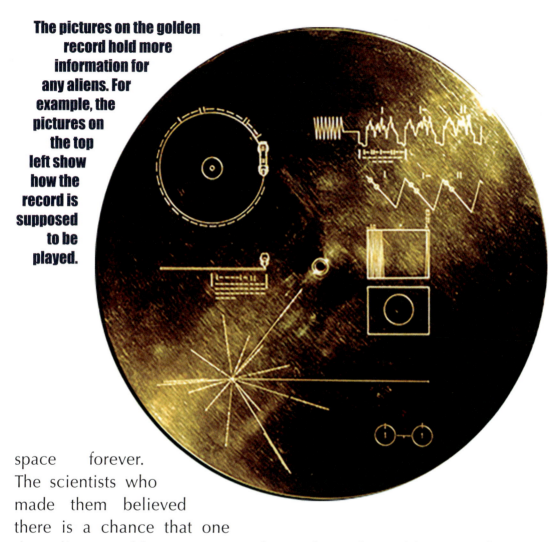

space   forever. The scientists who made them believed there is a chance that one day, aliens could come across the probes. The golden records are there to explain to any aliens who humans are and what Earth is like. They include animal sounds, greetings in more than 50 different languages, music, and more.

Since the 1960s, communications satellites have been built with solar panels on them. These help them use the sun's energy to power themselves.

EARTH'S ELECTRONICS

New satellites have been launched every year since 1957. Today, there are thousands in orbit. Even though the first satellites were meant for exploration, people quickly realized other ways satellites could be used. Private companies started sending their own satellites into space.

TV and Phones

Many people get their TV service through a company that uses satellites. The satellites send a signal to a satellite dish on a person's roof. The dish picks up the signal and sends it to the TVs in the house. Not everyone has satellite TV; some have cable instead. With cable TV, the signal is sent through large underground wires called cables. As of 2023, many people have stopped paying for either kind of TV. Instead, they use **streaming** services on the internet. However, many people still count on satellite TV for news and entertainment.

Fast Fact

About 75 countries have at least one satellite in orbit. Many countries have more than one, but many have none at all.

A satellite dish (*shown here*) can have trouble picking up a signal when it's covered in snow or ice, even if the satellite is still working.

Some phones and other forms of communication also use satellites. Most people use cell phones, which send and receive signals from cell towers on

SPACE JUNK

In 2018, an artist named Trevor Paglen launched a 100-foot (30.5 meter) reflective balloon into space as the world's first piece of space art. Paglen said his goal was to renew people's sense of wonder when they look at the night sky. In 2019, the satellite attached to the balloon shut off. Since no one can find the balloon, it's become just another piece of space junk.

Space junk is anything humans have left behind in space that isn't useful. It can include anything from satellites that have stopped working to tiny paint chips. In orbit, even small items move very fast because of Earth's gravity. Satellites and the International Space Station (ISS) could get damaged by them. This makes space junk very dangerous.

As of 2023, there are about 100 trillion big and small pieces of space junk orbiting Earth. Scientists are asking governments and companies to try to clean up the orbit before launching more satellites.

the ground. However, satellites can be used in places where there are no cell towers. This kind of technology helps ships and planes communicate with people on land.

Travel and Timing

The Global Positioning System (GPS) uses satellite signals to find the exact location of a point on Earth. People operating planes, boats, cars, trucks, and many other forms of transportation rely on GPS to help them find their way. If all the satellites in orbit suddenly stopped working, transportation all over the world would have many issues. Planes would have trouble landing, and trucks would have many problems carrying food and medicine to the right place. Drivers would have to go back to using paper maps. GPS can update instantly, but paper maps can't, so travelers would likely run into unexpected problems even if they did have a map.

Some traffic lights use GPS for timing. Satellites help them determine when to change color. Without the right timing, we'd have a lot more car crashes. Other things that use satellites for timing include some heating and cooling systems and power plants.

Credit card readers and banks also use satellite timing systems. If those satellites stopped working, people would be unable to buy things. This would be a big problem.

Satellites are also sometimes used to monitor, or check, what's happening on Earth. They might

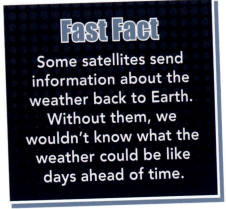

Fast Fact

Some satellites send information about the weather back to Earth. Without them, we wouldn't know what the weather could be like days ahead of time.

People who tell planes where to land are called air traffic controllers. Without satellites to help them do this, the planes might crash.

look for wildfires or oil spills to see how far the damage from them has spread. They can also be used to check for water and minerals underground and to help farmers better understand and manage their crops.

Satellites and the internet have mostly replaced older forms of communication, so it would be hard for people to send messages to each other quickly without satellites. Luckily, the people who take care of the satellites keep them in good working order. They make sure that their orbits don't decay and that they don't crash into each other.

The military uses satellites for controlling robots called drones.

Chapter Four

NEXT STEPS

New satellites are launched all the time. Some replace old satellites that no longer work, but most are for new things, such as business, science, and government work. Some people believe there could be as many as 100,000 satellites in Earth's orbit by 2030.

Satellite Constellations

Some companies have launched satellite constellations, which are large groups of satellites. One of the best-known is Starlink. This company is part of a larger company called SpaceX. Starlink's goal is to bring high-speed, **reliable** satellite internet to everyone in the world.

Starlink uses a newer, smaller kind of satellite called a CubeSat. Because these are smaller than older satellites, they can get closer together to cover more of the ground below. Starlink aims to put almost 42,000 CubeSats into orbit to meet its goal of providing

Fast Fact

A common way people deal with satellites that have stopped working is to allow them to fall back to Earth. Most of the satellite burns up in the atmosphere, but pieces of it do sometimes hit the ground.

REPAIR AND REUSE

Although scientists do often launch new satellites, NASA scientists would rather repair a satellite if they can than launch a new one. One satellite that is still working after many years is the Hubble Space Telescope. It was launched in 1990 and has taken many beautiful pictures of space since then.

In November 2021, the instruments on Hubble started sending error messages to NASA. A team of scientists spent about a month trying to figure out what was wrong and how to fix it. Hubble started working again in December of that year.

The Hubble Space Telescope has taken some beautiful photos of deep space, including this picture of a galaxy scientists call NGC 1097.

global internet. This is in addition to all the other satellites in orbit. Many people agree that everyone should be able to use the internet, no matter where they live. However, having so many satellites in orbit at once can cause problems, so Starlink needs to plan carefully.

From Earth, Starlink's satellite constellations look like moving lines of lights in the sky.

CubeSat Probes

Some scientists are working on ways to use CubeSats as space probes. They believe the best way to do this is to attach the satellites to solar sails. A solar sail is a thin sheet that uses solar wind the way a sailboat in the water uses the air's wind. A CubeSat with a solar sail attached would be cheaper to build and wouldn't run out of fuel as long as it's within the heliosphere. For this reason, they probably won't be used to explore interstellar space.

This picture shows one idea of what a CubeSat with a solar sail might look like.

Fast Fact

Solar sails may also make the CubeSats easy to steer in space. For this reason, they could be used to bring things to and from the ISS.

Upcoming Missions

While scientists work on the CubeSat probes, they're already planning other missions using different kinds of probes. On April 14, 2023, the European Space Agency (ESA) launched a probe to Jupiter. The probe, which is called the JUpiter ICy moons Explorer (JUICE), is going to fly past several of Jupiter's moons and take pictures. It will become the first probe in human history to orbit a moon other than Earth's.

Other probes will be sent to asteroids, Mars, and other moons. Mars is already home to several probes called rovers. These drive around on its surface, taking **samples** of the dirt and air as well as photos of the planet. Probes have changed a lot since *Sputnik 1*, and they're a key part of helping us learn more about outer space.

Fast Fact

One way scientists use satellites is to help them track the **migration** patterns of animals that are in danger. They can use that information to figure out what parts of the world need to be protected, or kept safe, for those animals.

This picture shows one of the Mars rovers, *Curiosity*, taking a selfie.

THINK ABOUT IT!

1. How might history be different if the Cold War hadn't happened?

2. What do you think would happen if aliens found the golden records?

3. How do satellites affect your everyday life?

4. What are some problems that could be caused by having so many satellites in space at once?

GLOSSARY

ally: A person or group that unites with others for a common purpose.

atmosphere: The thick layer of gases that surrounds a planet.

binoculars: A device through which you can more clearly see things that are far away.

breakthrough: A sudden advance in knowledge.

cosmic: Relating to space.

density: The amount of something in a particular area.

migration: The act of moving from one place to another at different times of the year.

particle: A small piece of something.

reliable: Trusted to do work.

remote: Far away from anything else.

sample: A small part of something that shows the quality of the larger item.

streaming: Playing continuously as data is sent over the internet.

technology: A method that uses science to solve problems and the tools used to solve those problems.

transmitter: Something that sends messages out.

Books

Bolte, Mari. *Roving the Red Planet*. Ann Arbor, MI: Cherry Lake Publishing, 2022.

Collins, Ailynn. *Probe Power: How Space Probes Do What Humans Can't*. North Mankato, MN: Capstone Press, 2020.

Murray, Julie. *Satellites*. Minneapolis, MN: Abdo Zoom, 2020.

Websites

BrainPOP: Satellites
www.brainpop.com/technology/communications/satellites
Watch a movie, play games, and take a quiz to test your knowledge of satellites.

Cosmos4Kids: Space Probes
www.cosmos4kids.com/files/explore_probes_space.html
Read more about past and future space probes.

NASA SpacePlace: Explore Mars: A Mars Rover Game
spaceplace.nasa.gov/explore-mars/en
Learn how scientists steer Mars rovers from Earth—and try it out yourself!

INDEX